P9-DWX-750

HANS

GREAT LESSONS
FOR A GREAT HUMAN
BEING.

WITH LOVE

BARB & TED

HAPPY BIRTHDAY

LIVE GOOD.

Compiled by Kobi Yamada
Designed by Jenica Wilkie & Steve Potter

COMPENDIUM™
PUBLISHING

live inspired.

This book is dedicated to all the good people; the world wouldn't be the same with you.

ACKNOWLEDGEMENTS
These quotations were gathered lovingly but unscientifically over several years and/or were contributed by many friends or acquaintances. Some arrived – and survived in our files – on scraps of paper and may therefore be imperfectly worded or attributed. To the authors, contributors and original sources, our thanks, and where appropriate, our apologies. —The Editors

WITH SPECIAL THANKS TO
Jason Aldrich, Gloria Austin, Gerry Baird, Jay Baird, Neil Beaton, Josie Bissett, Laura Boro, Chris Dalke, Jim and Alyssa Darragh & Family, Jennifer and Matt Ellison & Family, Rob Estes, Michael and Leianne Flynn & Family, Sarah Forster, Jennifer Hurwitz, Heidi Jones, Carol Anne Kennedy, June Martin, Janet Potter & Family, Diane Roger, Kristel Wills, Christy Wires, Clarie Yam and Erik Lee, Heidi Yamada & Family, Justi and Tote Yamada & Family, Val Yamada, Kaz and Kristin Yamada & Family, Tai and Joy Yamada, Anne Zadra, August and Arline Zadra, Dan Zadra, and Gus and Rosie Zadra.

CREDITS
Compiled by Kobi Yamada
Designed by Jenica Wilkie & Steve Potter

7th Printing. 10K 08 07
Printed in China

If we live good lives,
the times are also good.
As we are,
such are the times.

—St. Augustine

The dedicated life is a life worth living. Find something to love with all your heart. Discover what inspires your biggest dreams. Seek out a challenge that creates positive change, speaks of your purpose and makes a difference in the world. Throw yourself into something to believe in, that asks for your very best. We are here not only for ourselves: we are here to add to the sum of human goodness.

A good life is not lived by chance, but by choice. We can be wise from goodness, and good from wisdom. Each person brings into this world a unique contribution, and each day comes full of possibilities. All we need is time and opportunity; there is no such thing as an unimportant day. Our possibilities live as we live, and each one of us can bring hope and beauty to the world. Go out and find where people hold their potential and meet them there. Be not only good for yourself, but the cause of goodness in others. Inspiration and contribution go hand-in-hand. As Robert Louis Stevenson once wrote, "All who have meant good work with their whole hearts have done good work." Begin with life as you find it and make it better… anytime is a good time to do good.

BELIEVE IN YOU

Reach out and open the door that no one
thought could be opened. Life is behind it.

—Kelly Ann Rothaus

JRSeLF.

MAKE EVERY M

We don't have an eternity to realize our dreams, only the time we are here.

—Susan Taylor

OMENT COUNT.

SETTLE FOR MORE.

There is more in us than we know. If we can be made to see it, perhaps, for the rest of our lives, we will be unwilling to settle for less.

—Kurt Hahn

DO WH
YOU

AT LOVE.

Is the life I'm living the life that wants to live in me?

—Parker Palmer

EMBRACE

CHANGE.

Growth means change and change involves risk,
stepping from the known to the unknown.

—George Shinn

TAKE
CH

If you risk nothing, then you risk everything.

—Geena Davis

HANCeS.

BE

You must never be fearful
about what you are doing
when it is right.

—Rosa Parks

BRAVE.

FIND YOUR

You're only given a little spark of madness. You mustn't lose it.

—Robin Williams

PASSION.

GO WHERE YOU'VE NEVER BEEN.

Somewhere, something incredible is waiting to be known.

—Carl Sagan

Twenty years from now you will be more disappointed by the things you didn't do than by the ones you did do. So throw off the bowlines. Sail away from the safe harbor. Catch the trade winds in your sails. Explore. Dream. Discover.

—Unknown

HAVE AN ADVENTURE.

No pessimists ever discovered the secret of the stars, or sailed to an uncharted land, or opened a new heaven to the human spirit.

—Helen Keller

BE POSITIVE.

CREATE

If people never did silly things, nothing intelligent would ever get done.

—Ludwig Wittgenstein

BALANCE.

CELEBRATE DIF

THE

FERENCES.

It is never too late to give up our prejudices.

—Henry David Thoreau

Nothing ever becomes real till it is experienced.

—John Keats

SEE FOR YOURSELF.

TAKE NOTHING

FOR GRANTED.

Perform every act in life as though it were your last.

—Marcus Aurelius

CHERISH

I live for those who love me, for those who know me true.

—George Linnaeus Banks

FAMILY.

SHAPE THE
FUTURE.

Idealists, foolish enough to throw caution to the winds,
have advanced mankind and have enriched the world.

—Emma Goldman

Even if it's a little thing, do something for those who need help, something for which you get no pay but the privilege of doing it.

—Albert Schweitzer

VOLUNTEER.

MAKE SOM

eONE's DAY.

Too often we underestimate the power of a touch, a smile, a kind word, a listening ear, an honest accomplishment, or the smallest act of caring, all of which have the potential to turn a life around.

—Leo Buscaglia

BE A

Wherever we are, it is our friends who make our world.

—Henry Drummond

FRIEND.

WoRK

TOGETHER.

Problems can become opportunities when the right people come together.

—Robert Redford

MAKE A DIFFERENCE.

The difference between what we do and what we are capable of doing would suffice to solve most of the world's problems.

—Mahatma Gandhi

PRESERVE

NATURE.

Nature often holds up a mirror so we can see more clearly the ongoing processes of growth, renewal, and transformation in our lives.

—Mary Ann Brussat

STRENGTHEN
COM

YOUR MUNITY.

In every community, there is work to be done.
In every nation, there are wounds to heal.
In every heart, there is the power to do it.

—Marianne Williamson

LIVE WHILE

YOU LIVE.

Not to go out and do your best is to sacrifice the gift.

—Steve Prefontaine

CARE
DEEPLY.

What can burn and not burn up, a passion that gives birth to itself every day.

—Yiddish saying

The mind determines what's possible. The heart surpasses it.

—Pilar Coolinta

LISTEN TO YOUR HEART.

If you want to keep your memories, you first have to live them.

—Bob Dylan

CREATE

MEMORIES.

BE FIRST TO

SAY HELLO.

I've seen and met angels wearing the disguise
of ordinary people living ordinary lives.

—Tracy Chapman

LIGHT THE WAY.

Let nothing dim the light that shines from within.

—Maya Angelou

The world of reality has its limits; the world of imagination is boundless.

—Jean-Jacques Rousseau

THINK

BIG.

EXPECT

Determine that the thing can and shall be done, and then we shall find the way.

—Abraham Lincoln

SuCcEsS.

HAVE

FAITH.

I am not afraid...I was born to do this.

—Joan of Arc

We know what we are, but know not what we may be.

—William Shakespeare

BE NEW AND IMPROVED.

REDEFINE THE

Intense desire not only creates its own possibilities, but its own talents.
Don't be afraid to do something just because it's impossible.

—Kobi Yamada

IMPOSSIBLE.

BE THERE WHEN YOU'RE THERE.

Right now a moment of time is passing by! We must become that moment.

—Paul Cézanne

COUNT YOUR

We must find time to stop and thank the people who make a difference in our lives.

—Dan Zadra

BLESSINGS.

My hope still is to leave the world a bit better than when I got here.

—Jim Henson

LEAVE A LEGACY.

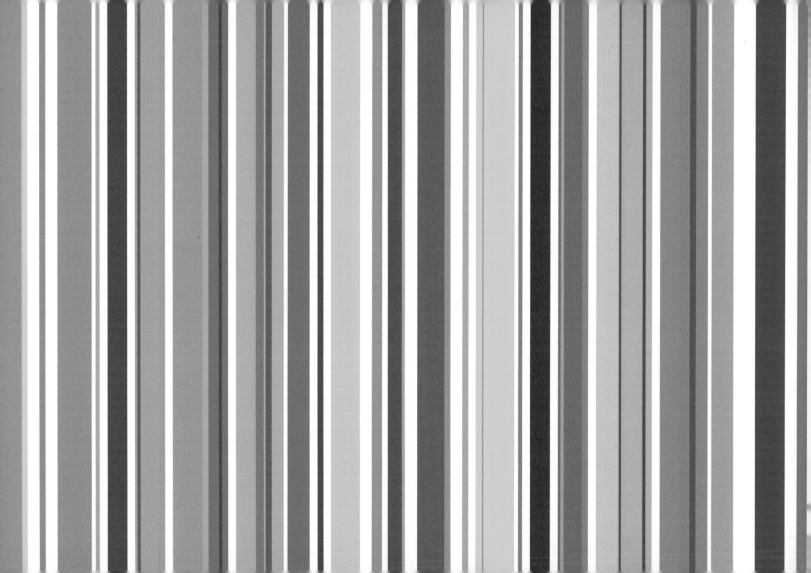